HEAVY METAPHOR

HEAVY METAPHOR

POEMS

by

R. Macdonald

Heavy Metaphor

Cover design arranged and formatted by R. Macdonald, with guitar graphics designed by Ezepov Dmitry; used by permission through Shutterstock. Other cover design elements by Canva; used by permission.

FIRST EDITION

Library of Congress Cataloging-in-publication Data is available upon request.

ISBN: 9798673853023

DISCLAIMER

This is a work of fiction and whimsy. Characters, events, situations, scenarios, and incidents are either the products of the author's imagination or used in a fictitious manner. Any resemblance to actual persons, living or dead, or actual events is purely coincidental.

Poems that are based on actual individuals or events are identified in the end notes. Details have been changed to protect the privacy of the individuals.

Before criticizing political correctness, please read the end notes for explanations and references to historical works.

DEDICATION

To my wife Blenda, whose love and relentless hard work provided me with the time and head space to pursue the expression of my art.

Often a hard life

requires a hard starboard.

TABLE OF CONTENTS

FOREWORD

My life has been a perpetual compulsion for creative expression despite lack of training. I did take some piano lessons, but I never learned to read music notation. That did not stop me from composing music and songs. My enjoyment of poetry was sparked during the academically undemanding years of high school. Things changed during my college training in science, and I developed a sheer terror of all literature coursework. I had to keep an A grade average in order to get into medical school. My science mind could not compete with the students who majored in liberal arts subjects. They were very eloquent in their class participation and term papers, and they set the standards for what a student A grade was. Once, one of my poems was used by a professor as an example of what not to do, and I experienced one of the worst social humiliations that I have ever felt. Thereafter, I avoided any class that would put my creative writing under scrutiny.

After my professional education was complete, my free time became consumed with discovering the things on which I had missed out. The self-abnegation of necessity became the gluttony of lack of consequence. I began reading the text of Shakespeare plays, and found joy in what previously would have been a career goal-ending impediment. I also subscribed to poetry magazines and read poetry critique. However, I did not like most of the modern poetry I read, and I let my subscriptions lapse.

In my new safety of the personal realm, I felt compelled to write. In poetry, I saw a beauty that I felt just had to come forth from me. It was a hobby never meant for academic critiques or approval. My grandmother had written poetry to show family members, but she never bothered to try to publish. Our poetry was akin to secret family recipes never to be shared publicly, passed down only by blood.

Eventually I got the courage (or arrogance) to submit my works to poetry publications. Overconfident, I chose prestigious magazines to consider my poems, and time and time again I was rejected—typically without explanation or by template response ("...it has merit, but...").

One day I received some much-appreciated feedback about why I was being rejected. I sent a poem called "Pairs Figure Skaters" to a publication called Wild Goose Poetry Review, and for once I got a real human response and explanation. The reply read as follows:

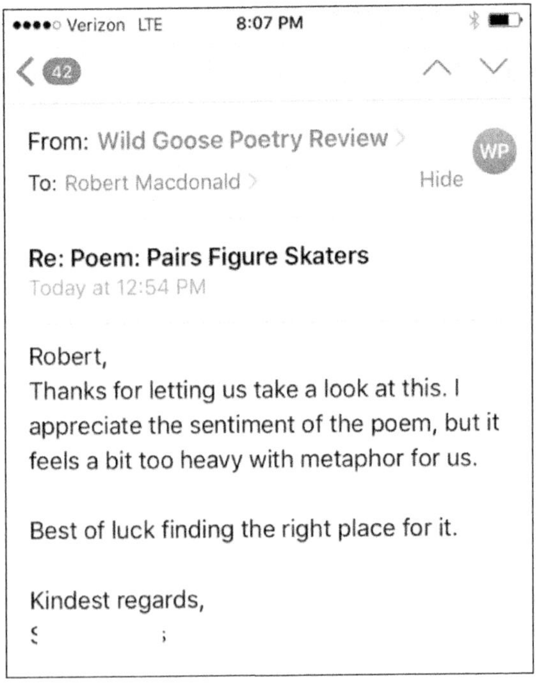
●●●●○ Verizon LTE 8:07 PM

42

From: Wild Goose Poetry Review

To: Robert Macdonald

Hide

WP

Re: Poem: Pairs Figure Skaters

Today at 12:54 PM

Robert,
Thanks for letting us take a look at this. I appreciate the sentiment of the poem, but it feels a bit too heavy with metaphor for us.

Best of luck finding the right place for it.

Kindest regards,

My responding thought was something like, "Heavy with metaphor? Heck yeah, exactly the way I wanted it!"

I have learned that the world of poetry criticism is a blood sport of the elite that takes glee in insulting and punishing nonconformists and less than genius work. Authors' online customer feedback book reviews are plagued with pompous put downs meant to brag about the reviewer's educational credentials and perfectly discerning taste in what constitutes "real" poetry. Every literary age has standards by which work is judged, and failure to abide typically results in rejection, failure, and oblivion. Occasionally, disregard for the rules results in posthumous recognition or a new movement that becomes the toast of academia and the art world—temporarily followed by voluminous imitation. It seems to me that the current tacit rules for poetry include that there must be novelty, wording minimalism, left justification, rhymelessness, and near-prosaic format. Poetic content is to exist at the poles of subtlety and unexpected jolting originality, with the in-betweens seen as banal. The heavier poetic tactics are considered antiquities to be admired, but not to be emulated. I break rules constantly, and similar to Eliza in *My Fair Lady*, I am a vulgar barbarian in the court of modern poetry. I frequently stack different metaphors in the same poem, pack words densely into phrases, use commas and hyphens unapologetically, engage in hyperbole and whimsy, and have the occasional audacity to rhyme.

I have noted a poetry trend that I call "nonsensical novelty." In contrast to the paradox and emotive non sequiturs of Pablo Neruda and others, these elements seem to be placed with the sole intention of never having been written before. I consider it to be the splatter painting of poetry—randomness that is imbued with nonexistent meaning.

I prefer the classic logical metaphor strategy that has the ability to resonate within the reader regardless of time and fashion. Fashions so frequently look stupidly embarrassing in retrospect. In the 20th century, music composers often wrote atonal novelty pieces that pleased critics but have never become works that people want to hear repeatedly over time. Enduring music structures are loved because they appeal to something deep and inherent within us. The poetry that endures by attracting voluntary re-reading will inevitably be structured in accordance with human nature, not the whims of fads and critics.

I am more than a little rebellious to the notion that nothing past can be revivified through personal experience, digestion, and viewpoint. I love the styles of the past, and I have nothing to say using the current rules. I love classic poetry and heavy metaphor for the high potency drugs that they are.

Any repetition of previously used metaphors or phrasing is unintentional and only due to my ignorance of the millions of poems that I have never read. I confess that my due diligence against replication is time and effort limited to a one- or two-page Google search. I make no claims that my poems are original in any significant way, but they work for something deep within me. I love to puke them out, and they are exactly what I want to experience in poetry. The creative process keeps me buzzing with something in my head to which I cannot say “no.” I frequently experience time warping flow states which are consuming and addictive. On days that I don't engage in creativity, I feel like something is wrong.

I caution that it is likely that anyone indoctrinated with a BA or MFA in literature will not enjoy this book. It will be emetic putrefied kryptonite to PhDs and professors. My word gumbos are meant for minds free of literary zeitgeist, and who might catch the same buzz from them that I get. I don't write to please critics, and I no longer have to get A's.

Defying truth is like defying gravity:

both result in a splattered soul.

PAIRS FIGURE SKATERS

The music begins,

Moving ripples of limbs,

Spinning mere humans into seraphim,

Skimming ballet pirouettes and unwinds,

Their backs arcing blindside to passage of time,

Aerial flight paths that break earthly ties,

Angelic steel wings caress pages of ice,

Inscribe the carved surface,

Love letters in cursive,

Ineffable verses,

Love letters to life.

MEDITATION ON THE ANGELS

As I focus on my breath,
my lungs rhythmically filter
the warm vapor of L.A. air.
Lotus flowers do not grow here.
I meditate upon the deep concrete scars
that drain the tectonic high-rise crust.
This is the new nature:
the symbiotic crush
of flesh and exoskeleton—
a xeriscaped coral of living people
inside their stucco husks—
a great reef that rakes the carbon sky.
The strongest blooms of color
are the scattered crime scenes with
their red and blue pulsar lights—the urban
rainbows of human darkness refracted off
the streets of desire.

The dandelions dare to peek out
from their sidewalk crack doors.
In blind faith, they release umbrellas
to the rainless fuming yonder.
Airborne, they parachute into the melee of
man’s quaking creation.

BREEZES AT TEN THOUSAND FEET

The fever breaks 'neath perching tundra.
Aspen trees are scoured and strummed,

Ten billion notes in presto tones,
Commence the grand September scrum.

Vivid yellow coruscations—
Sparkle rain of quaking leaves—

Drop celebrating ticker tape—
A Jackson Pollock strobed caprice.

Ten billion hands, as one, applaud
The vernal win and dog day feast.

Ten billion kiss earth's autumn lips,
Bedding down the tumbled scree.

Before the falling crystal dew
Precipitates the thin air scents,

Let sit and stir in blustery whir
The sifted down ingredients

Of summer's cauldron
Cooled to sleep

By breezes at
Ten thousand feet.

DOG DANCE

Released into the yard,
the small dog runs at
flank speed with focused intention.
He flickers unpredictably as a fish in the depths
weaves together the light beams that connect
heaven to the primordial slime.
He is a darting kite in the sky of grass
tracing an unseen maze.
He drafts the angles of canine
geometry obtuse and acute—
the floor plan of the Temple of Wolves—
the edges of Lawnhenge and its
alignment with the firmament.
Each change of direction:
the secret steps of a ritual ballet
conducted by earth, wind, and fire.

At the perfect spot in perfect compass,
a sudden stop—a pose statuesque,
plié, and balancé.

All acts mundane in the
pilgrimage of life
are sanctified when
performed in accord
with the perfect unseen
sacred order.

HEAVY METAL

Timbred with thunder,

guitar seismic clouds

rain sonic attacks

from Valhalla to ground!

An electrified razing

of pick shredded strings

blasts voltage stacked airwaves

on crowds stoked to sing.

Distorted notes thrash

their gullets and brows

with staggering riffs

firing bullets of sound.

A tribe unifies with

a fist forest raised

and head banging ritual

to join the rave

to the spotlight fantastic's
spectacular squalls
and industrial hammering
by steel williwaws!
From Valhalla's arena,
existentialist fog
is cleared in the now by
the lightning of song.

SUMMER FIELDS

On baked and brilliant days I go,
Stepping through the
Knee-high grass—

Snapping, dry,
Beige, and
Brittled.

Daisies sway and ricochet.
Dandelions burst
In fireworks.

Grasshoppers leap
Like popcorn
Popping at my feet—

Each stride alive with
The ordnance of
Summer fields.

HER HUSBAND'S SUICIDE

Only a ring now remains,
No beginning,
No end.

His embrace was replaced by the
Suffocating squeeze of bereavement.

Photographs kaleidoscopically stare.
Wishes and pleas fill regret heavy air.

Makeup and tears color pillows and sheets.
Mascara graffiti paints murals of grief.

With no note to explain or chance for good-byes,
The half empty bed holds a sleepover of "why?"s.

Every day is a circling procession of
Pain so relentless and unanswered questions

That orbit her senses

Like the ring that remains,
No beginning,
No end.

NIGHT SURGERY

A lone porchlight
flicks on and smolders upon
the farthest frontiered northern night.
It is welcomed with the
fluttering fanfare of a throng of moths
sent leaping from the grassy
fringe of darkness.
They sweep and whorl
in powdery flight paths frenetic.
They swing on their sorties
and make looping knots.
They suture and swathe
the light to the dark
soothing the wounds made each time
the night bleeds cool black
on the creation-tattered
backside of the world.

STORMS

Perpetual sunshine
dries fields and withers growth.
All who come to this place
are asked to toil
in mouth-deep mud
and till souls with the
thunder and floods of storms.

Those who only face the sun
never gaze upon the rainbow.

PRISON LOVE

When there is no one to love,
at least you can try to find
someone to humiliate.
For a moment,
the pleasure can be difficult
to tell apart.

DEFORMED INFANT

You were a tiny arc

in the circle of life

necessary to keep

the rest beautiful

and strong.

☯

WISHING WELLS

As a child, Jane kept a penny jar.
She threw pennies into a
wishing well to petition the angels that
she was told were all around her.
Once she wished for a doll in the toy store catalogue—
the desirable one with the pretty deluxe eyes
that open and shut with movement.
Her parents were on welfare.

Nothing came.

The pennies rusted in the darkness
of the well just as dreams rust into
the lightness of awakening.

In 8th grade, Jane threw pennies
into a wishing dryer, shut the door, and
turned it on hoping to create a spark
in that clattering crucible of yearning
and to telegraph pleas to the angels who
were apparently hard of hearing.
She wished for the beautiful eyes of the women
in the bleachers of newsstand shelves that
watched her in the store.

Nothing came.

The angels stood silent, apparently preoccupied
with greater tasks in the tumbler of life, and
she remained unattractive and unpopular at school.
The dings in the dryer rusted red—
as did become the eyes of her angry mother
on discovery of the damage—
as did Jane's face from the

corrective beratement in front of her sister.
Her mother confiscated the penny jar and
exchanged all the pennies for paper money at the bank.

At age 25, Jane visited the Grand Canyon.
She wished for her eyes to see a sign—
a revelation from the angels on how
a better life could come into being for her.
She threw pennies over the edge and watched
them vanish from sight, never making a sound.

Nothing came.

With time and the lightness of awakening,
she learned that angels merely bear witness to what is,
and their job is not to procure and polish dreams,
but to allow rust to color canyons and
lives excavated by the river of life.

In those depths is where
wishes belong.

ANGER

noun

an·ger | \ 'aŋ-gər

1 : A negative hostile emotional state.

2 : Instant devout faith that malevolence has breached the social contract.

3 : A strangling seizure of dissatisfaction.

4 : A flailing protest to the cold cosmos
that shrieks the antonyms of *namaste*
with turpentine teakettle tongue.
It strikes as lightning
illuminating its own source:
the liminal rawhide
between persona and the
dark terrain of mind.

5 : The orgasm of perceived injustice—
unstoppable once begun—
a flooding consumption—
a cresting wave that
rifles its rider through
a muzzled barrel
onto the sandpaper shore
abraded with each reprise.
Those at its mercy are
driftwood whittled naked
by the boiling riptides of the
primordial gasoline.

CHRONIC PAIN

A labor that births itself,

The worship of relief,

The preacher of nihilism,

A manifesto for disbelief,

A scorching black serum,

A mathematical proof,

The Siddharthan theorem,

Undeniable truth.

TIME

Time: The precious commodity that cannot be grasped, seen, admired, hoarded, or displayed for boasting.

Time: One is born wealthy then becomes incrementally poor.

Time: Is constantly and inexorably spent, either wisely or prodigally. All sales are final, and there are no refunds.

Time: Its own thief in the commerce of life.

Time: Dealt in the casino of velleity.

Time: Squandered in the pursuit of soul poisons.

Time: Sliced away by the dual scalpels of sun and moon.

Time: The improvised symphony notated by thought, word, and action; timbred by individuality, syncopated by mistake, dissonant in hubris, flourished by triumph, without intermission, always incomplete.

Time: Warped by the special relativity of
situation—slowest in misfortune and
misery; fastest when well-spent and
synchronous with the divine conductor.

Time: A coiled path pocked by the vanity of
happiness, glee over the suffering of
others, the mishandling of the soul.

Time: Commemorated by the renewal vows
and rings of the tree's marriage to forest.

Time: Clocked by hourglass sand grain falls;
plumes of sunrise; the pulse of starlight
sparkle; moments of eye contact; shared
touch, smiles, and laughter; the scrapes,
cries, and giggles of children.

Time: The most valuable alm one can give.

Time: The only thing by which human love can
be measured.

Time: Let each day begin with the fall of the
last grain in mind.

Time: May each last grain fall into
the hand of God.

THE CYCLIC RED CIRCUS

The righteous stood up for justice.
They steeped the masses
And fomented a tea of their collective resentment.
All were made to drink,
And like a miracle diet aid,
It shed the pounds of abundance,
So that all were leveled by austerity.
Hunger for equality was traded for hunger for food.
Compassion became a magician
Who made both luxury and subsistence vanish
Before awestruck crowds.

Step right up!
Watch the next performance!
Each MC has a new attractive costume
Concealing jealous flesh that sweats bitterness.
See how the humane become tyrants,
Solidarity raises another army,

Manifestos of progress become

The script of the apocalypse,

And equity becomes the smiling reaper

That ushers all into the big top slaughterhouse.

NIGHT IN LAS VEGAS

An inverted night—downside up,
neon stars sprinkle the earth and
shine their light up into dark heaven.
Countless lighthouses on vertical shorelines
beckon each ambling ship
on the concrete currents
tacking the luminiferous aether.
Their courses wind erratic as
their spirit animal—the moth—
intent on the beguiled plunge
into blinding light.
Guided by the Braille of desire
on the map of 'nows',
they sail into
the sparkling noir.

WOMAN WALKING

Primal as the serpent's slide,
Tilting hips in measured stride,
Brassiere cups harness her power,
Straps—her reins that steer the hours.

Casting shadows—fleshen shade,
Peaks and valleys, tidal waves,
Citrus drop and marmalade,
Swells astern, perfume grenades.

Stilettos stab the sidewalk straits—
Calipers that navigate,
And chart her course into the deep
Currents of ancestral sea.

MAN ON CHRISTMAS EVE

I.
Three wee cards upon the T.V.
Join his celebration and
Toast a seventh cider.
Far away, another man
Plays with his children.

II.
The flashing lights, red and white
On pines within neighboring windows
Crown halos upon angels of urban fog—
Mirthful mocking beacons warn of
Black ice on the edges of life.

III.
The frozen phone lies dormant
Hibernating in the unbearable
Lightness of silence.
The refrigerator, the winter within,
Snores indifferent at the winter within him.

IV.
He trips and twists the radio switch,
Slashing across the wavelengths till
Jolly tunes parole his mood and
Hemorrhage cyclic sameness
Over the cold moments.

V.
The shining knife, icy bright,
In the kitchen drawer winks—
Offers to lead by the hand
To a dance under the mistletoe
And a kiss on the neck.

VI.
A scarlet scarf falls in *au revoir*.
Torment forms a poinsettia pool
That reflects a now resting
Merry gentleman, and a soul
Lifted from all restraining orders.

MIGRAINE

Rainbows portend the quickening
of the storm—not its end.
The sparkling fuse
ignites electric hail—
a scouring squall of
kundalini lightning over
Hell's concert blasting
detuned heavy metal through
plutonium amplifiers.

The skull miscarries
the cares of the day
as the breech litter of pain
kicks in demand for a midwife.
Denied, a riot flash floods
the grey streets,
looting the hours, in search of the
apothecary of dream
and seven grams of slumber
in the soft dark arms of
silence.

METHAMPHETAMINE

Day and night intertwine
A hurricane of chaos and order.
Time suspends patiently
On the cusp of euphoria.
A calliope of plosive elation
Plays in a parade on
The streets of despair.
All the worries the future hurls
Deflect harmless into the
Gutters of the perfect now.
The wife of anniversary ennui
Becomes the bride of the urgent honeymoon.
The kiss splintered by decay is veneered
With the minty fresh of new desire.
A tsunami of content washes
Clean a life stained by expedience.
All 'musts' prostrate to the
Temple of Hedone.
For now, fireworks light
The dark crypts of a
Life built on the
Sands of the
Hourglass.

VAMPIRE

It is painting oneself into a still life.

It is the orchid mantis whose arms clutch the hours.

It is the Buddha's twin never leaving the pleasures of the
palace.

It is pressing the lever that kills the caged rat.

It is the vanity where the stage make-up is never
complete.

It is an awake coma.

It is the next prison term of the repeat offender.

It is the drowning pool of Narcissus.

It is the luminous lure of the angler fish.

It is perpetually shaking an unthrown *I Ching*.

It is the kleptomaniac never expelled from the household.

It is being trapped in the eye of the Yang.

It is running a treadmill during the Battle of Marathon.

It is strength training for breaking the 10th
commandment.

It is suicide by sweets.

It is blindfolding the third eye.

It is a rehearsed kiss never planted.

It is an opium den with a revolving door.

It is beholding flowers through a welder's mask.

It is borrowing pleasure from a loan shark.

It is an atraumatic quadriplegia.

It is bulimia for placebo.

It is admiring a dessert case that spoils the supper
appetite.

It is chain-smoking before one's execution.

It is a magnifying glass for studying the sky.

It is the rabbit hole where all things say, "drink me"
but never quench.

It is the thesaurus of mistranslation.

It is an oath to a dictator.

It is a time machine that transports to one's funeral.

It is self-insertion into *The Matrix*.

It is a vampire at the neck, unseen in the mirror.

THE EMPTIED SPACE

When a child is born, the womb empties
and a different space is created in the parent:
a cavity wherein the child seems
to live and grow.
It is excavated throughout
the body as tunnels—deep veins
coursing parallel to the
circulation of soul.
It is their playground.
It is where they return after school.
It is the space where
the air of their laughter
respires within.
When a child's eyes lose their light
and wilt into the opaque
grey stare of infinity,
it becomes an empty tomb

where memories ricochet
from the firing squad
of grief and regret.

We are pieces of one another,
never complete—
a mixture of elements
tumbling as an aggregate that
shapes the concrete of our being.
Our destiny is to have
spaces made
by the exit wounds
of loved ones.
Though haunted,
those places
make room for
something new
to grow.

RAIN IN LAS VEGAS

A cool blows in
as casinos wheeze,
the raindrops land,
the asphalt steams.

•

Marriage vows
spill forth in vain
as fleeting as
a virga's rain.

•

Electric laughs
of hope machines
mock the clonic pulls
the patrons seize.

•

The odds are gods
stone deaf to prayers
that evaporate
in smoke-filled air.

•

Though fortune knows
the skies will clear,
what comes here comes
to disappear.

AMERICAN TO A HAGGIS

Glare foul—your godless glossy case,
I fill with fear to know your taste,
You seem to be a toxic waste,
Cold, fried, or warmed;
I'll push you past my loathing face, for
Here it's the norm.

My groaning gullet now is filled,
With curds of innards, oats, and swill,
You stretch my gizzard to the gills,
I'm gonna bleed;
Gawkers know I will be ill,
That I concede.

I rinse the taste with Irn-Bru,
And raise my head up high to you,
Surviving well the Scots milieu,
Proudly I rave,
My faith in Scotland now renewed,
Food o' the brave!

ONE WITH THE TIGER

Such a curious way to meet you,

From stranger to dinner guest,

To fall from the heights of the captors,

To the lowly gates of hereafter.

I press my hands together and

Acknowledge your divinity

And the oneness of our atoms

Forever churning in the fathoms.

Hypnotized by the hurricanes

Twisting in your eyes,

I see that the universal appetite

Must be satisfied.

Our zero-sum hunger for infinity

Requires something to die

And strengthen the bones of being.

The living stand on the graves
Of those willing to surrender
Everything to the darkness.

And so, I say a
A prayer to my slayer,
My mantra—your menu,
"*Namaste*," says your entrée.
Bon appétit,
Goodnight.
I will sleep tight
Under the majestic sheets
Of the dark matter
Mattress of creation.

GRAND CANYON

The sculptor's chisels are
flashflood and trickle
patiently hammered
precise to the dimensions
of the sky's mercurial mood.
Cutting through the canvas of ancient oceans
raised up on high in praise of the maker,
the friezes form a monolithic cathedral
from earth's blood bidden to run
through the distillery
of the quantum gruel.
A slashed pallet of reds stack
from the sacrifice of stone.
The walls echo endless,
the wind their witness,
the sung call-response of
the cosmos to herself.
The river winds westward
in search of the ocean who calls
for her great-great-ancestors to return, asking,
"Let our colors reunite."

KARMA AND THE WRITER'S WIFE

A writer's wife walks the lonely path.
At the end of the wedding aisle, bride and groom
part ways and walk alone,
hidden into distant thickets
dense as krill-filled baleen—
their lives whales apart.

She is a war bride, her man deployed
to the vast no one's land, missing in action,
periodically found and furloughed to special occasions
that bring folded love of greeting cards
from anonymous substitute authors.
Each request for human contact:
an assault on the art,
a derailment of flow,
a divergence from
somewheres the artist must go.

It's not like she imagined—a pleasure world
of creative unfolding, spectacular word winds
and phrase waves lapping at the
Venus shell of her regal pedestal.
Instead, silence…
a distance logarithmic to inspiration's slippery slide rule.

He is inattentive, angering...with acquired deafness of an
embattled gunnery sergeant hooked on fox-hole
adrenaline—his nor'easters of inspiration,
her maddening dead calms.

She was so attracted to creativity—
a compelling gravitational force
that pulled her into the
whirlpool wigwam heat lodges of passion.

What if she had married a rock guitarist?
There should be a household clamor of distorted chords
morphing into order before her very ears—
sonorous fanfares summoning future success—
watching quaking banks rupture money upon
the fault lines of fame.
In reality, the ad nauseum sound is a wall
as impenetrable as the writer's silence—
the distance as real—
the deafness even deeper—
his fingers callused from fretboards and metal strings—
their touch stony—rough upon her breasts—
his eyes distant upon groupie muses
of imagined nightclub harems.

What if she had married a painter?
...to watch his breath hover over the canvas void then
speak, "Let there be color!"
...as with brushes he conducts the tempests that bespeckle
blooms across white linen deserts to fashion paradises
found—only to find rejection as never the object of
portraits—always banished from the Edens of his oils.

If the writer succeeds, money makes the distance
grow and the cell blocks more solitary.
For the first book she won the crown
for the dedication page pageant,
but she is only an invisible runner-up in books thereafter.
The accolades feel empty.
They are not meant for the supportive spouse
who is relegated to scavenge in the dark for
leftover scatters of limelight.

The typewriter is a marriage breaking machine
that chops vows into word scat and Scrabble letters
on a game board of truth and consequence.
The rage of the forsaken brings pitchforks and torches
to a connubial crucible.
Rejection begets revenge.

The war of art wreaks collateral damage,
and that which attracted becomes that which repels.
That which was desired becomes that which disgusts.
To the delight of everyone minus two,
the fire of art burns brightest when its fuel
is the immolated artist crackling alive
with the hell fire of neglected love.

MUSIC

Art is war against our separation.
Music is that war's most powerful weapon.
It melds minds with magnetic air.
If shared, the collective unconscious
may be pulled from the darkness of the deep
and rise to awareness through
bombardment by the artillery of notes.

All music can be hymns to each other
as divine beings in life's oneness.
By joining in the chorus,
we may erase our spotted past,
and the spotted staff becomes
the strands of the DNA of peace.

WAITING FOR TRANSPLANT

The ache and the breath arise gripping and one.

A down counting timer his heartbeat becomes.

His teeth gnash and clamp on hysterical tongue

That prays for the death that will dissect the young.

The prostrated guilt of the beggar goes numb,

For his hand is not out for mere bread, but for flesh.

Like the vulture he waits for a life to divest

Into feast that will fuel him to soar from his bed,

And rise from the fallen to Phoenix and then

To live before greeting this dying again.

CODE BLUE

The man's heart beats, stumbles, and falls into
flatline—the short tightrope between
timed life and timeless suspension.
Hands are bone-crushing pistons on his sternum—
an outboard motor aiding the failing
engines of animation.

Lightning bolts across his chest
and the thunder of splintering ribs
frighten and delay the earth from
gaping wide its grim lodge.

I pause to look at his blue face—
wobbling side to side from the beating—
seeming to say "no"—
his pupils blown wide open with a pleading diameter—
between the geometry of nowheres and novas.

A higher power called mercy overcomes
and flows down through me.
I raise up a hand and summon angelic hosts
to swaddle the last artificial breath then set it free.
I announce the time that proclaims
passage of the invisible
through the invisible
to the invisible.

I write an epilogue in his chart.
Preparing to inform his family,
I don a white coat as if a ceremonial robe.
I enter the room where they have been waiting for word.
Everything stops.
Their eyes lock onto mine…
I become the ocean that takes in their tears.

THE FISH'S HEAVEN

Released from the deep blue
ghettos of murderous anarchy,
of famished feast or frightened flight,
of sushi banquet or watery casket,
it is nirvana where only smaller fish
exist and swim helplessly hobbled—
willing filleted food stocked
league-deep in the wide-aisled ocean grocery
for the supper buffets of eternity.

DEPRESSION FREE FALL

The dream movie house lights go on,
The final scene fades away,
Like a reverse fainting spell, dark into light.

The long wait then begins—
The gauntlet of hours
Between the ceasefires of sleep.

Tasteless breakfast—
The first communion
Of excruciation.

All matter stops mattering.
Days fill with antimatter
That repels the substrate of being.

Strafed by meaningless moments,
A metronome of numb
Keeps time in the skull.

The small tasks of the day
Loom colossal in the way
Like gatekeepers shoulder to shoulder.

A long-whiskered face
Abrades the grindstone
Of earth's slow turn.

The colors of day—
Faded lackluster stains from the
Wash cycle of recurrence.

The spouse in the other room
Signed a contract of non-disclosure as
A powerless magician

Whose spell words of
Nuptial vows failed
To conjure the promised bliss.

The workday's cast of people
Look like they're on the other
Side of shower glass—

Morphing opaque forms of
Black and grey watercolors
Running down the blotter of the day.

Each secondhand tick is a
Hammer on the anvil that bends
Upright posture into fetal.

When new art courts your attention, why bother?
They are just the same color swatches
Shuffled from the deck of yesterdays.

A stare down with foods of the fridge—all tried.
Why bother when they'll tell your tongue
What it already knows?

Unattached...it's what you become effortlessly.
It's the goal of some religions, but it's
Yours without adherence to a discipline.

You are the mottled leaf
Wind-ripped from the tree,
Free-floating debris adrift from source.

And then the countdown begins for
Return to the mattress—
A capsule to orbit the

Side of the earth where the sun cannot
Scrutinize the dream script in which
All scenes unfold

In your favor, and all
Your lines speak of the short
Victory unconsciousness brings.

REAL LIFE

Who lives the real life?
Each generation reincarnates the
compulsion to discredit the one before.
The rebellious refuse norms as inauthentic.
They morph their appearance with pendular
regularity and claim to be free of mandates.
They update and rebadge the titles of their tribesmen:
bohemians, the avant-garde, beatniks, hippies, rockers,
punkers, free spirits, revolutionaries, anarchists, burners,
the 'whatevers'. Many are the names of the avatars of cosmic truth.
They melt the old idols of prestige and recast them in their own image.
Within the safe hallucinations of perpetual youth
they rail against the pursuit of wealth, social values, and conformity
as costumed charades on a potholed stage of vanity—
all false goals in a tangential race
ending with a barbed finish line that
entangles with fiction and fantasy.
They see themselves as untethered exemplars by
working for subsistence,
dwelling in conspicuous contrast,
donning novel appearance,
rabid consumption of pleasures…

In a sleight-of-hand trick of preposterous hypocrisy,
artificial chemical consciousness is
declared superior to the natural human state—
a blasphemy that unzips the codex of creation,
detonating the nuclear rage of the gods.

Unfortunately, there is a problem with the authentic life:
it is no more authentic than any other,
and reality persists regardless of what we think about it.
Age, decay, and disease
return everyone to the center where
they are forced to gaze upon
the unsplittable building blocks of being
and the monetization of life.
Pain is a landlord that leases out bodies then
unpredictably returns to demand payment.
It accepts only money and penalizes
the empty-handed with multiplied suffering.
Neither wealth nor poverty can buy happiness,
but money can appease the great equalizer that is pain.
The only authentic lifestyle is that which
accepts meaning beyond care-free youth,

confronts pain eye to eye,

properly negotiates an agreement,

ponies up, shakes hands,

and smiles.

ANGELS

They appear without fanfare
Of trumpet or horn,
Summoned by call lights
And scrub suit adorned.

They're haloed fluorescent
By ceilings of light
And float room to room
In a hurtling flight.

They perch on the siderails
To guard and assess
Beneath saline storm clouds
That rain into flesh.

Needles they plunge
In a sharp healing touch,
And anoint life-strafed wounds
With wings gilded in gloves.

They are not the message,

Just souls alongside

Assisting the burdens of

Short precious life.

THE ENDLESS FEAST

Glory, glory! The jubilee has begun!
Sound the commencement horns
for the feeding frenzy upon the
cornucopia of industrial capital's
machinery of multiplicity.
Let in the light,
Let no can or cabinet contain its darkness.
Open the gates,
release the krakens of appetite!
Millennia of ancestors cheer
the harvest of perpetual food—
a dream for which they prayed
daily to the harsh gods of earth and sky;
for they finally have heard the
critical mass of prayer and
cracked open mother nature to
erupt volcanoes of alimentary magma.
Sugary manna falls from the sky
to ice each pantry into Krypton's
crystalline phantasmagoria.
"Glory glory!" they sing from the graves
while their children's children now
dig their own deeper with each mouthful.
Finally, the bounty has arrived.
The cargo cults' prophecies are all fulfilled.
It is the harvest festival of 365 days,
no season, no end, with every vomitorium
leading to the entryway of the next feast.
The steam shovels of modernity
lay waist to the fields of famine.
The old gods are expelled, and a
new liturgy of malignant gratification begins
as the two-handed communion is dozed
into the vacuuming funnels of fury.

"Glory glory!" cheer the ancients of the savannahs.
"Glory!" they sing from sepulchers of shale.
The sausage train runs day and night:
bowels filled to fill bowels.
Hand over fist over hand over fist,
we are fattened for sacrifice to our own achievements.

No one knows whether the revels will end
in a cataclysm of meteor, sun fire, religious terror,
or the return of Marxist dystopia.
For now, let the living know satisfaction supreme, and
the dead envy the swollen bodies interred beside them.

SOUL MATE

/'sōl ˌmāt/

noun

1: Disillusion's thrilling overture.

2: A fiction that rots the tomes of the ancestral stacks.

3: A sewage of the factories of romance.

4: The toxin that poisons the soul insatiable.

5: The courtship mirage that vanishes upon approach.

6: The idea that, if wedded, annuls to the recessional.

7: A hallucination from the street drug of fairy tale beginnings.

8: A dream's slow disease that festers the daylight.

9: The gullible heart's inevitable infarction.

10: Doubted when one is only gifted bouquets of child vomit in toilet bowl vases.

11: Cupid's gangrenous arrow wound.

12: The hot hookup ever alluring, ever abandoning.

THE DEADLIEST SIN

Envy is the deadliest murderer

to ever walk the earth.

It roams and witnesses successes

and sees only crimes and trespasses:

Shakespeare was a thief stealing money from actors and audiences.

Henry Ford was a mosquito sucking blood from factory workers.

Oprah ransacked the assets of her fans and advertisers.

A mansion is a mugshot of a criminal,

a luxury car—a getaway vehicle,

a fur coat—a felony.

Envy is an organism—

a transmitted virus infecting

its hosts with rabid killing rage.

It is the perpetual plague afflicting mankind—

the original disease.

From Cain to communism,

the murder spree marches on,

outrage pocked and unappeased.

HIGHLAND LULLABY

Twinkle, twinkle,
Dew that's sprinkled
Far across the moors,
Heather sways
By River Spey,
Enthroned above the shores.

Sunlight briefly
Strokes the sheep we
Watch as day recedes,
The grasses drink
What falls and sinks -
And then they go to sleep.

RIME OF THE WIVES' WEATHER

Red sky in the morning,
husbands take warning.

Red sky at night,
husbands take fright.

Red sky at noon,
misery comes soon.

MAKING OMELETTES

You have to break eggs to make an omelette.
You have to break people to make a utopia.
Violence is the required ingredient.
Blood is the sauce that brings the best taste.

It is the excuse of every chef of revolution past.
Oh, glorious cookware of gulags and gallows
that feed the resentful masses.
It can't be wrong when the result is so beautiful.

Nothing ideal is born without labor pains and blood.
Let the corpses of the unwilling stack
to build the victory arches
and fuel the ovens of exaltation.

"Thou shalt kill!" command
the gods of societal perfectionism.
Their priests respond, "Kill we shall,
for the living seekers of paradise
have a hunger for death never satisfied."

EMPHYSEMA IN EMERGENCY

The frail striated man struggles
and sucks upon the nebulizer
like a frenzied fish on a boat
gasping to conjure sea from parched sky.
He is trapped between the moments of an
infant's first breath of life struggling to devour air
and a dying man's failure to pull in
just one more.

Perched forward,
jailed behind the rails of his bed,
he is sentenced for arson of his lungs.
Under the brier of webbed tubing,
he is Ahab tied against his nemesis,
submerging and surfacing,
choking on the swells,
preparing to spit his last breath—
just one more.

Through the white clouds of sheet and mist,
his thought stumbles back to a younger day…
inhaling the breath of a lover's mouth,
her body weightless in the suspense of his rounded arms,
the only thing heavy—their desire—
his world endless in the promise of her surrender,
telling her countless times
while kindling a cigarette,
"Just one more."

An alarm rips him from the respite.
Summoned back to the gallows,
he will ascend to heaven, an inch with each
chin-up of the diaphragm,
and break the tethers of phlegm

that ground him from the effortless place
where angels and nicotine
make no demands for
just one more.

ADDITIONAL EYES

Most people are born with two eyes.
Some have one additional—
a third unseen eye that perceives
the metaphysical scaffolding of being
and the divinity of humans.
You seem to have six additional eyes
that perceive the calculus of power
and the utility of humans.
They are arranged as jewels in a crown.
You are royal.
You hold court in your nest
and see in all directions.
People are statistics in your ledger.
You spin a web of smiles that
conscripts each person of value
into the serfdom of friendship.
Your tongue wraps them in silken kindness
and mesmerizes with flattery.
You digest their insides
and sip them in—
cannibalizing their human energy.
You molt to expand your
coffer of luxury.
You rule with eight orbs
and build castles from
the dry husks of your prey.
Yours is a kingdom
of human *mâché*
and convivial
venom.

All life is triumph!

LITURGY FOR THE DEPRESSED

Priest:

We pray that sleep lost to soul poisons
be regained by the stillness of the night's
natural order.

The people:

May it wash suicides to where they drown
unbereaved.

Priest:

We pray that the prisoners of electronics be
released by real relationships.

The people:

May it wash suicides to where they drown
unbereaved.

Priest:

We pray that the carbohydrate termites of the
brain be replaced by Earth's natural soul foods.

The people:

May it wash suicides to where they drown
unbereaved.

Priest:

We pray that the avoidance of pain and strenuous
activity be replaced by acceptance and
commitment to them.

The people:

May it wash suicides to where they drown
unbereaved.

Priest:

We pray that universities be purged of the heretics of the blank slate blasphemy.

The people:

May it wash suicides to where they drown unbereaved.

Priest:

We pray that the nihilism of the Cult of the Sourceless Universe be replaced by the meaning brought by living in accordance with the sacred source of all things.

The people:

May it wash suicides to where they drown unbereaved.

All:

Amen

THE BEER'S PRAYER

Our Lager,
Which art in tavern,
Swallowed be thy foam.
Thy kegger comes,
Thy will be drunk
In mirth as it is in tavern.
Give us this day our ale-y head,
And forgive us our emesis,
As we forgive those whose emesis is upon us.
And lead us not into incarceration,
But deliver us from beatings,
For thine is our income, the hours, until morning,
We haver and haver,
Barmen!

See end notes.

WOULD YOU RATHER?

Would you rather die of a stroke or a heart attack?
Would you rather die in the slow strangle of
an anaconda's throat, or rapidly shredded
in a piranha feeding frenzy?
Would you rather die in agony
watched by a vigil of loved ones,
or in the bliss of a morphine drip with strangers
watching the clock to strike shift change?
With three children, or three published books
positioned around the death bed?
Ripe and comfortable with eyes averted to atrocity,
or young and tortured in defiance of it?
During ecstasy with a stripper,
or during the misery of a marital crisis?
Would you rather painfully live then die,
or painlessly never have lived at all?

The perfect death is a legendary beast
that is never encountered—

an explorer's fruitless quest—
a sailor's tale to entertain by lamplight—
a bedtime story before the big sleep.
Life is a terminal disease without a cure, so
we tell stories of diversion as respite from awareness.
We take flights of fancy above the noble truths,
then land and think them the injustice
of a psychopathic god.
The lottery of life at once
awards and revokes its jackpot.
Like urban gang life,
the only way in is blood,
the only way out is blood.
We are all conscripts of a gang called Being.
The secret is that to ever
have had blood at all
is a triumph that is the
envy of every star
that ever was.

NOTES TO STILLBORN TWINS

Mommy:
There was only a week until you were due.
Did you have Pinocchio dreams?
You didn't need to, because briefly you *were*
real live boys, nothing wooden—just tender flesh,
bitty noses, tiny fingers.
Did you hear the music I played for you in the car?
Did you hum along with my shower songs?

Daddy:
Did you know that your nursery was
completely furnished and decorated,
ready to welcome you?
Mom chose the colors; I did the painting.
Your baby shower items still sit in the closet—
your ultrasound pictures still hang on the wall.

Mommy:
Did you speak liquid words to one another
like dolphins and whales?
Did you play thumb wars?
Was your nocturnal karate to waken me
to console your bad dreams?
Were you excited with anticipation
of your birthdays and fireworks of first light?

Daddy:
Did you fear that on the outside
your first breaths would feel empty
compared to the dense hydraulics
of mom's dark atmosphere?
I wanted air to flow into you
directly from my gasps of joy
at beholding you.

Mommy:
The doctor said it was random that you died,
unpredictable, unpreventable.
Forgive me if my body was too weak to nurture…
if I lacked vigilance.
I know it's not true, but I feel like I should have known
your kicks were to tell me all was well,
and that their absence was your quiet mayday call.
We know it was a good death.
You died in your sleep, right?
Just after dreaming of seeing the faces that talked to you
through my muffled tummy telephone… right?
My last words were not an argument with
your father for not helping me enough… right?
I'm sure they were "I love you"
before that silent good night.

Daddy:
It was the worst day of our lives.
They delivered you in parts, your limbs
too fragile when pulled, bones too soft…
The sound of the ripping was the worst
thing I have ever heard.
At least neither of you could hear it.
Like toy models they reassembled you
to present to us for viewing. We grieved over your
parts, attempting kintsugi with our tears.
We joined you as shattered beings—all of us the same.
When breezes blow through our fragments
they will be windchimes calling your names.

Mommy:
You have changed substance and now live in us as pain.
It is better to have you with us that way
than to have nothing left at all.
I will hold you both in my spirit forever.
You are eternal in me—I am your heaven,
and I welcome you through my gates.

THE 10 SACRAMENTS OF THE DEMONS[1]

I. The Initiation
Scattering marbles on the floors of a blind person.

II. The Cinemockation
Humiliating someone while filming them on a phone. Post on internet.

III. The Schattenfreudestation
Sending hate for the deceased to a grieving mother or father.

IV. The Entrepreneuriot
Rioting for a "cause" to loot or steal from those envied.

V. The Transmogrification
Placing thalidomide in the meals of an expectant woman.[2]

VI. The Exculpation
Justifying the use of "any means necessary" to accomplish an end.

VII. The Nazification
Proclaiming collective guilt or inferiority of an enemy group.

---

[1] With the exception of the Exultation, sacraments may vary according to Earth era, scheduling constraints, and or per discretionary jurisprudence of Beelzebub.
[2] May substitute placing a potent carcinogen in the french fries of a child.

VIII. The Hatrecourse
Intercourse with a hated enemy group's woman. [3]

IX. The Radikillization
Killing out of devoutness for one's ideology.

X. The Exultation[4]
Killing out of devoutness for one's religion.

---

[3] A.k.a. the hate breed of the demon seed. Higher unholy rank for multiple conquests/victims. Incubi may substitute standard rape and escape. Succubi see DL manual of exploitation and physical and mental castration of enemy males.

[4] Satan himself presiding. Après ceremony complimentary libations, followed by decapitation kickball, severed handball, then paradise dance rave, BYO.

TOILET BABY

After a flail of physiques,
you were the aftermath
of a failed physics exam—
the tailpipe byproduct of a careless
undouched Tuesday hookup
pumped and dumped—
the fetus that survived
only to rappel into a
prom night toilet bowl:
baby-flavored punch perfectly apropos
to the "under the sea" themed revelry.
You locked gaze with mom for an instant
and saw mercenary hedonism
as she denied you the breast
and instead force-fed you
the swill of unflushed indifference.
While you were still stunned
with the first light blinding,

mom ran to trip the light fantastic
as she trickled afterflow on the dance floor
to spell out "Buzz off, it sucks to be you"
to the groove of her favorite song.
Her lactation-ready cleavage
was proudly displayed before
awestruck fondle-ready pimpled urchins
unaware that its divine sustenance
would soon be pumped and dumped
into the sewers of adolescent calamity.

After a nine-minute life,
you drifted into cold eternity
interred three feet below
the swinging waste bin lid,
covered with the paper towels
that washed mom's hands clean
of feckless teen maternity.

SCRIPT OF THE YOUNG WOMAN'S TATTOO

My cups were filled.
My period was an exclamation point.
My diploma was a laurel held up high.
My blemishes were painted over with makeup
into a self-portrait emulating female ideal.
But...something is wrong.
My mother failed to initiate me into completeness.
I am not window dressed on Main Street
but instead scattered—
a cheap yard sale in a remote cul-de-sac.
My prestige,
my rank in the whispering order,
my title in the hive
are questioned by the Morse blinks
and skullward glances of the social monarchy.
To remedy, I enter the
vogue cathedral of collective yearning
and proclaim my readiness for ordination.
I examine the sacred book of symbols
and choose which will be mine.
The ceremony is performed by an
illuminated piercing-clad priest
using a needle crosier, holy ink,
and wordless crackling electric incantations.
I endure it without whimper or tear.
He anoints to a sheen my blisters.
I make the heroine's journey and
return with the stigmata to prove it.
My re-blemished body testifies that
I have crossed the threshold of womanhood—
fully assembled—a zenith female
whose moonlight fills the theater of shadow.

DISCLOSURE

Beneath the leap of hope
into a shallow pool of friendship
lie sharp stones that
slash and dissect.
A bloodshed of silence runs
over the face of pretense,
as disclosure sounds the depths.
When the waves of regret smooth
and resurface the mirror,
there casts the reflection…
an unmasked clarity,
a fallen gaze refusing to behold,
fear below the surface,
holding its breath,
hiding.
The waters chill
and tremble.

PUNISHING THE ABUSER

Mere storm debris in a father's drunken fury,
the boy was tossed by wrath-wrapped words
and love-bare knuckles.
The barrage blew to extinguish all sparks
of disobedience and childhood magic.
Now compliant, the child cowers in
the fuming ass crack of the room,
summoning the resentment
that will bellow the payback
tempests of his manhood fists.
Only a pound of flesh can
atone for a pounded flesh.
Only another's pain
can assuage his own.
Diamonds form only under crushing pressure,
and it must be that relentless hammering of being
will forge a broken life into wholeness.

Karma is real;

and what was begets what will be.

Violence clones itself in the

lab of human transgression.

TATTOO POSTSCRIPT

I am still incomplete.
I need another…
and another…
and another…

I am incompletable.
Each gouge of skin plants seeds
that sprout new needs.
Each stroke of ink writes
segues begetting segues—
questions whose answers pose questions.
I am the book whose illustrations
obscure the cover and the story.
I am paying a tailor to weave a cloak.

This pilgrimage to self-illumination
is chasing the unreachable sunset
whose light casts long shadows.
Each stride toward completion is merely
the suspended step of the crane.

HEAVY METAPHOR

The belts of the best
writers are displayed
in libraries across the world—
the trophy cases of mental brawn's
hard fought wins on the
gridiron of the gods.
From pages, they still speak the
transcendent lexicon that
warps all tongues unto the
vortex of creation.

But professors, fearful and pretentious,
warn never to challenge the forebears
in their weight class, for so many
poets have fallen mangled
unto the wannabe killing fields
of the scholarly mind chipper.
They coach the generations
to duck and dodge
the impact of phrases past,
the combinations of syllable and sound,
stunning rhymes of dizzying precision,
and incising words of weaponized diction
from champion bards throwing
the mighty fists of heavy metaphor.

PUNISHING THE ABUSER 2

She was a victim that coped.
The young girl that was violated by secret invasions,
negotiated her silence in exchange for favors:
sweets, toys, dolls, trips…
Her abuse became a business.

With childhood behind her,
she transformed from victim to victimizer,
and now her enterprise continues.
She lives before other adults
extracting favors, exploiting them,
always trying to compensate for
what was lost by that girl.
She turns on the waterworks like a faucet:
tears of extortion and compliance enforcement.
Her spouse and friends become substitute pedophiles
who must atone for what happened to her.
With each person she tacitly asks, "What do I get?"

She is suing this existence for reparation of damages,

because it is a criminal that she will bring to justice.

Karma is real;

and what was begets what will be.

Abuse clones itself in the

lab of human transgression.

Note: This is based on a real person and a true story. I by no means blame the victim for their abuse or the damage they sustained.

PHYSICIAN A.W.O.H. IN PANDEMIC

The virus swept in like a particle storm,
leaving people dead by thousands multiplied.
We physicians stood there frightened.
Donning masks, gowns, and gloves like
armor before battle, we reported for duty.
At roll call, silence fell after your name.
You didn't show up. You managed to get the other
doctors to cover all of your duties,
and take the risk of death upon themselves instead.
Months passed, and all you did
was shelter in your mansion cowering alive
as other doctors died of the plague.
With your doctorate of medicine, you were given
wealth and status by society in exchange for protection,
sanctuary from suffering, or just to be
footprints in the sand.
Here are words you uttered before witnesses:

> *"...I will remember that I remain a member of society, with special obligations to all my fellow human beings, those sound of mind and body as well as the infirmed. ...If I do not violate this oath, may I enjoy life and art, respected while I live and remembered with affection thereafter..."*

On Olympus you professed that oath
to mankind and the gods, or whatever
higher power above may be,
to be the servant of the health and lives of humanity.
Instead, you made an oath to serve
your own health and life.
Rather than being a refuge for others,
you built a refuge for yourself with earnings
from the conveniently sick who posed no threat to you.

Your wealth became a citadel that kept
the plagued people outside your gates.

What if a firefighter abandoned his team and fled
from a massive forest fire,
leaving some of them to burn alive?
At fire's end, would he still be permitted
to call himself a firefighter?
Would he not transform into something else?
...a fire flee-er?

When a soldier in war runs away to save his life,
he is AWOL and considered a deserter. In cowardice,
he increases the risk of death of his fellow soldiers.
He is a criminal who is stripped of rank and is executed
for one of the highest crimes
that a soldier can commit.

You committed one of the highest crimes
that a physician can commit.
You are a deserter in the battle to save lives,
and you fled in your luxury vehicle to save your own.
There are no soldiers to arrest and
return you to face justice.
There are no medical courts to
prosecute and strip you of your degree.

You went absent without honor—AWOH—
the crime we barely remember existed
since the black plague ended.

I hold you in contempt and feel shame for our profession.
Amongst our ranks are those whose profession
is harvesting cash only from the harmlessly infirmed.

May the gods show mercy in the place
where those go who break oaths, desert, and
leap off of Olympus with wings of money.

COUNTDOWN OF FIRSTS

The opening of the eyes that see a first light.
The doctor's first utterance of, "It's a..."
The first drying of the body.
The first taste of a mother's liquid meal.
The first fall of toddling.
The first heart broken.
The first regret.
The first child.
The child's first inkling of parental imperfection.
The first line of the face.
The first gray hair.
The first lick of a fingertip for grip.
The first insult from a son.
The first page held at arm's length.
The first permanent bodily pain.
The first gray hair of a daughter.
The first death of a friend.
The first heart attack.
The first breach of urine.
The first taste of a factory's liquid meal.
The first fall with inability to get up.
The first drying of urine-soaked clothing while
awaiting help.
The doctor's first private conversation with the
adult children.
The doctor's first utterance of, "time…"
The closure of the eyes that see a second first light.

YEARBOOK MESSAGE TRANSLATIONS

Stay cool this summer!
I don't know what to say to you. I will speak in default uncertainty mode as if you will matter in my future.

It was great having you in class!
I know that you only asked me to sign your yearbook to pack its pages with evidence of your popularity, but perhaps my name in your yearbook will increase mine.

Too bad we didn't have classes together this year. Maybe next year!
I auditioned for a role in your life, but sadly I am relegated to this blurb in your credits.

Keep in touch this summer, dork!
I wish I could spend time with you to show you how worthy I am of your affection.

It's been great goofing off with you this year. Don't be like Ms. Walters, hahahahaha!!!
I was jester to your royalty, and I earned my keep with jokes and self-deprecation. Thank you for allowing me in the court of your lunch table.

Later days.
Goodbye meaningless relationship.

You da' man! Stay awesome bro!
I bow to your adolescent power and present my jugular.

I can't wait to get out of here and on to college!
Our friendship is as shallow as the ink on this paper. But that's OK, I guess. This becoming is necessary costume play—masked in acne and confidence—a dress rehearsal for the debut of the real performance.

DEAD MARRIAGE

He was provider, protector,
playmate, paramour,
co-conspirator of an ecstatic revolution—
now stripped of roles except
for the provider part.
A man marries and works for money
to pay for shots at the high-stakes
carnival games of procreation.
She is now the jaded carny who closes shop,
and redirects him to the fattening food stands
and nowhere rides of starting line arrivals.
Each day he requests a swing
at the high striker—each day denied
as if by the irritability of perpetual menses.
Her eggs dangle as stuffed prizes out of reach.
She shudders to his self-centered
woo-less advances with low-grade disgust—
his moves all memorized—
predictable choreography

on a dance floor grind of odors,
sweat, and sap—
the dread experience a mere smothering damp
assault on her torso—a pollution.
When her man is away, she fantasizes
about letting other men play the game
to clamorous bell rings of cathedral grandeur.
He fantasizes about outings to new fun-fair frolics,
with thunderous Thor-like swings of his hammer.
Her desire is bottled, capped,
under pressure, volatile—
her recipe locked in a vault.
He is thoughtlessly flatulent,
inappreciative, unaffectionate
…that is, until his urges throttle
and he becomes a bumbling locksmith—
a clumsy hacker.
The avoidant wife reinvents herself as platonic
bread winner or maid then resents the role.

The inconsiderate husband mechanizes into a
eunuch robot in a factory of the material—
a cash machine withdrawn from daily.
Careless love breaches the marriage contract
and shreds the promissory notes
of the courtship love letters.
Instead of making romantic gestures,
they become mutual blood letters
and maggots on the nuptial corpse
that once thrived alive to a fleeting joy—
destined to transform into flies
yearning to buzz off to imagined
elsewhere dung heaps of hope.

FALSE HUMILITY

The mansion: it's not mine, it's owned by the bank.

The luxury vehicle: it's the best crash protection for my children.

The exotic vacation: I needed quality family time.

The nanny: they help me spend time on the important things.

The home theater: I didn't want one, but it came with the house.

The weekly massage: it's the only way I can handle my stress.

The flamboyant gown: it was on sale.

The net of jewels: they were a gift.

False excuses spackle a foundation

of makeup masking the

creases clawed by the climb

to the throne

of power.

DISCLOSURE BETRAYAL

Disclosure is confession that attempts
to offload the burden of secret imperfection.
If the friend who receives it
did not want the weight placed on them,
they transfer it to as many others as possible.
The betrayal of confidentiality becomes mockery.
The mocked sinks in status,
as the mocker insinuates their own superiority
as if free of defect.
Disclosures become a ladder to ascend.

Beware those who profess wholeness
and perfection, for they will not allow
your blemishes to stain their costumes,
your woes to encumber their spines,
or your faults to go unclimbed.

SPLATTER RANT OF THE ORACLE

My check brain light went on,
so I presented to the oracle
for a deluxe psychic systems analysis.
She received me into her antechamber
and probed my pockets for loose ego.
She skimmed my passwords and hacked my firewall.
She gripped my head and began to speak.

She said that
counterculture hatchets upon my dry vines where
cocaine dust storms stripped away the grapes of joy.

She said that
a viscous rancid drips upward from my stalagmites of
soul spotting the Sistine vaults that separate
the light from the darkness.

She said that
my Buddha nature uses all synthetics
as it bathes in petroleum hot tubs on the Sunset Strip
high and low on heroin and robo-hookers.

She said that
my attention to current events is split
as Half-and-Half poured over
morning flakes of newspapers tossed on
suburban southwest porches.

She said that
I am an epileptic of misgivings
that stands on the ledge indecisive
with one foot in the hokey pokey of suicide.

She said that
my hesitation marks are a barcode that
scans for slashed rock bottom prices while
I hemorrhage resilience down the drains of
human flourishing.

She said that
I am a nomad dung beetle of modern life
rolling amassed worthlessness through
serendipity deserts and mirages of meaning.

She said that
technology is a serial killer that drops napalm and toxic
psalms on jukeboxes, board games, hopscotch-chalked
playgrounds, and landscapes explored by the
tenderfeet of wonder.

She said that
artificial intelligence and natural stupidity byte down
on the throttles that inhale meaning
and moon dust from the animistic atmosphere.

She said that
city blocks of computer chips creep their ghettos
into dark downtown alleys where their
ringtones multiply storms of mange and
melancholy into palm-sized silicone sarcophagi.

She said that
I am lost—the toss that traces a gutter ball trajectory
errant into sewer drain stagnance or stuck in high
branches near plastic shopping bag banners of treetop
kingdoms.

She said that
I am the chew toy of diseases which gnaw upon
fast food clad bones towards the marrow—
the deep core where prions plot invasions
into cold-cut reptilian contentment.

She said that
I have a lead deficiency
and recommended an aspirin, an apple,
and hot buckshot showers in perpetuity
for my cranial pangs for existential appetizers.

She said that
I am exploding in reverse—
the splattered leaper that launches skyward
to reassemble into a single seamless flesh
only to become a self-immolating monk
hungry for 15 seconds of char-blistered fame
on a social media with no followers or cause.

She said that
my elevator pitch to St. Peter is stuck between
floors as I paddle my tongue incontinent
over the karmic abyss of cables.

The oracle's fingers fanned a deep-fry inferno—
scalping and scorching me into a never-mind
tinder bliss of psychic incineration.
Spilling from a dustpan casket,
my ashes stain the oracle's guestroom bed sheets.
She hangs them out the window to the
pugilistic cheers of meat-hooked feminist lynch mobs
circumambulating the bonfire of the humanities.

SOULICIDE

Soul poisons

always

taste good.

†

RHYMES

Sometimes
Rhymes
Conspire
To kill a poem,
While the poet labors
Unaware and deaf to the words
Whose lyrical screams arise
From the page to make
Mellifluous music—
An elegy to thoughts buried
In the shallow
Grave of paper.

SNOW CHARIOT

I am light—
A particle and a wave.
I slice through the white matter
Dividing the Yin from the Yang,
Blasting contrails of comets.

I am dark—
Nothing and nearly everything—
The black hole that spins the blinding galaxy around me.
This is the hunt passed from my forefathers
Inside the deep caves of initiation.

It is the chase of the wilderness beast
That poises to destroy or give life,
Pulled by the gravity of physical existence
And its desire to complete its journey to the
Destined endpoint of being and time.

Flanked by an
Avalanche of angels,
I snap the reins of my chariot,
Hurtling unto
The breach.

END NOTES

1. Breezes at Ten Thousand Feet
This is about fall color change of the aspens in Colorado.

2. Summer Fields
I grew up in southern California where summers are the dry time of year for grasses, though flowers continued to bloom.

3. One with the Tiger
Inspired by an actual incident at a zoo in India in which an observer fell over the exhibit's edge into the tiger habitat. After a tiger approached him face to face, the man began verbally pleading or praying and repeatedly making the *namaste* hand gestures. After observing the man's petition for several minutes, the tiger seized the man's neck into its mouth, dragged him away, and killed him.

4. The Beer's Prayer
This is my version of a meme of unknown origin. I altered it to better mimic the original prayer upon which it is based. Though there are variations, this is a typical prior version:

Our Lager which art in barrels,
hallowed by thy drink.
Thy will be drunk, I will be drunk,
at home as it is in tavern.
Give us this day our foamy head,
and forgive us our spillage
as we forgive those who spill against us.
And lead us not into incarceration,
but deliver us from hangovers,
for thine is the beer, the bitter, and the lager
forever and ever,
Barmen.

5. Notes to Stillborn Twins
Based on actual horrific events experienced by an anonymous couple. The content of the notes is purely fictional and based on my own imagination of how severe the pain could have been. In no manner is the content meant to represent the actual thoughts and feelings that they experienced. Some details have been changed.

6. The Emptied Space
For H. L. Sutherland and family.

7. Man on Christmas Eve
An imagined backstory to an actual Christmas Eve suicide.

8. Angels
The message referred to is that life is painful and short.

9. The 10 Sacraments of the Demons
The Hatrecourse refers to numerous historical examples of using feigned loving intercourse or genocidal rape as a weapon for ethnic/racial/religious cleansing. Examples include slave owner rapes of slaves, the Nazi soldier rapes of Jewish women in Poland and elsewhere, the Rape of Nanking by Japanese soldiers, the Pakistani army rapes of Bangladeshi women in the Bangladesh Liberation War, the Serbian rape camps of the Bosnian War, the Muslim Boko Haram abductions of Nigerian Christian girls, and too many others to list.

10. Tattoo Postscript
References the film *The Suspended Step of the Stork* directed by Theodoros Angelopoulos. No, I am not against tattoos.

11. Physician A.W.O.H. During a Pandemic
This poem is purely fictional. Characters are either the products of the author's imagination or used in a fictitious manner. Any resemblance to actual persons, living or dead, is purely coincidental.

12. Dead Marriage
This refers only to marriages during reproductive years, and it does not necessarily apply to later companionate phase marriages.

13. Soulicide
I thought of this term, but my subsequent research found that it had already been coined. As far as I can determine, the term soulicide was originated by a cover band named Soulicide. This poem is not a reference to the band, but I credit them with the term. At the time of this writing, I could not find evidence that the word was trademarked or proprietary.

14. Woman Walking
This poem is strictly about an attractive woman's sexual power over men. It is not a treatise on every positive aspect of womanhood, intellectual power, general social power, maternal power, or any other aspects of women. If you want the whole story, please read an encyclopedia and calm down.

15. Prison Love
I do not condone prison rape or any other criminal activities perpetrated in prison.

16. Snow Chariot
To Honor!

ABOUT THE AUTHOR

Raised on welfare by a poor family in California.

Joined the U.S. military to pay for college and medical school.

Became an emergency medicine physician.

Got married and had kids.

Got out of the military.

Became an emergency metaphysician.

Composed music.

Wrote poems.

Ascended and descended mountains.

Not dead yet.

Printed in Dunstable, United Kingdom

67280515R00078